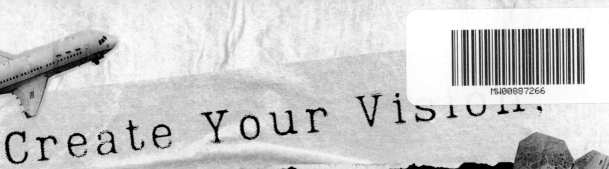

# Create Your Vision,

# Celebrate Yourself

Welcome to your Vision Board Clip Art Book for Black Women, a book lovingly crafted to inspire, motivate, and support you in creating the life of your dreams. Inside, you'll find images and words that reflect a wide range of life's aspects, from dreams and goals to values and relationships. Every page is designed to help you visualize and manifest your unique vision.

As a woman, you are a powerful and creative force. As a Black woman, you carry a wealth of culture, resilience, and beauty that deserves to be celebrated every single day. This book is your safe space, filled with visuals that represent who you are and who you want to become.

Use this book to craft a Vision Board that captures every facet of your life: from career to family, from travel dreams to self-care. There are no limits to your creativity! Cut, paste, compose, and bring to life a masterpiece that will be your daily reminder of what you desire and deserve.

Are you ready to embark on this journey of discovery, inspiration, and growth? The pages are ready, and so are you.

**YOUR FUTURE IS WAITING—START BUILDING IT TODAY!**

Meal Plan

| | | | |
|---|---|---|---|
| Sun | | | |
| Mon | | | |
| Tue | | | |
| Wed | | | |
| Thu | | | |
| Fri | | | |
| Sat | | | |

STAY ACTIVE

EAT HEALTHY

EXERCISE

SLEEP WELL

KEEP THINGS SIMPLE

THINK POSITIVELY

HEALTHY FOOD

eat less sugar

MEAL PLAN

PLANT BASED MEAT

Drink more WATER

I'am helpful

Lose weight !

NO EXCUSES

Fitness

GYM

I AM Strong

Exercise EVERY week

NEVER GIVE UP

#NO LIMITS

you can Do it!

SPORT

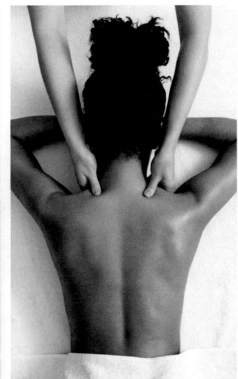
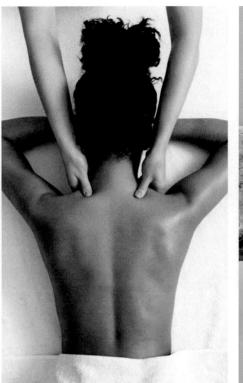

Don't FORGET · TO · RELAX

SELF CARE

Stay Focused!

LOVE MYSELF

Self-care IS EMPOWERMENT

# family is EVERYTHING

*Wedding*

**SUPER' MOM** ♥

*love* ♡

BOY OR GIRL

*You & Me*

*sweet moment*

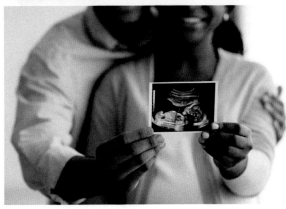

partner in CRIME

WHO RUNS THE WORLD? GIRLS!

THE FUTURE IS FEMALE

FRIENDSHIP

Be Happy!

GRL PWR

TOGETHER WE RISE!

BLACK POWER

Better together

YOU ARE CAPABLE

YOUR ONLY LIMIT IS your MIND

home sweet home

HOME

DREAM

LUXURY

LIFE

Dream Big

WORK IN PROGRESS

SAVE

INVEST

DEBT DEBT FREE FREE

$

FINANCIAL FREEDOM

positive

ENJOY YOUR LIFE

goal

FUTURE

FOCUS

SLOW DOWN

CHANGE

PRACTICE MIND FULNESS

IM POSSIBLE

Practice GRATITUDE

CAN'T CAN

FOLLOW YOUR heart

everything will be OKAY

SLEEP 8 Hours a Day

DON'T GIVE UP!

BELIEVE — IN — YOURSELF

Don't Be SO HARD on YOURSELF

make YOURSELF a PRIORITY

All THINGS are POSSIBLE

Live what you LOVE

Pack Your Bags

NEVER stop EXPLORING

LOS ANGELES
TOKYO
NEW YORK
SÃO PAOLO
LONDON
PARIS ROME
FRANKFURT
DELHI
MOSCOW
TORONTO

TICKET
TICKET

time to TRAVEL

Wander
The Earth

HAPPY JOURNEY

EXPLORE the world

TRAVEL

Adventure
Memories

Ready For NEW ADVENTURE

MY life IS Nomadic

HOLIDAY

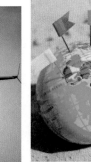

# ITALY

 MEXICO

 JAPAN

 SPAIN

 BKK BANGKOK

 SYDNEY AUSTRALIA

PARIS

 MOROCCO

BRASIL

GERMANY

 PORTUGAL

I ❤ ICELAND

Hawaii

OSLO NORWAY 23/09/17 DEPARTED IMMIGRATION OFFICER

 Malta 28.06.2017 IMMIGRATION ABCD 0123 DEPARTED

LONDON

 5

 RUSSIA MOSCOW

NEW YORK CITY

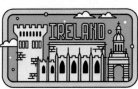 BULGARIA

 INDIA

WELCOME TO Fabulous LAS VEGAS NEVADA

I ❤ AMSTERDAM

 ROMANIA

 IRELAND

 CANADA

 CROATIA

 BARCELONA SPAIN

 BELARUS

 NETHERLANDS

Argentina

Chile

Bolivia

 CERTIFIED PRODUCT · MADE IN VIETNAM 100% ORIGINAL · PREMIUM QUALITY

LAOS

 GIZA · EGYPT PYRAMIDS

Indonesia

TÜRKIYE

 REPUBLIC OF THE CONGO

JAMAICA

SOMALIA

TANZANIA

SENEGAL

SUDAN

RWANDA

I ❤ SIERRA LEONE

SWAZILAND

UGANDA ZAMBIA ZIMBABWE TOGO

HOBBY

EXPLORE NEW IDEAS

Be Creative

CREATIVE WORKSHOP

CREATIVITY

CREATIVITY

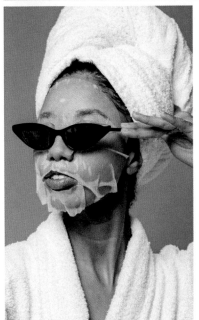

# FASHION

NEW · NEW · NEW · STYLE · STYLE · STYLE · NEW · NEW · NEW · STYLE · STYLE

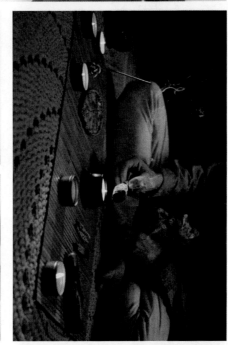

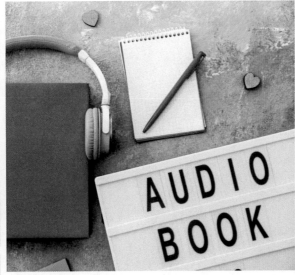

**AUDIO BOOK**

**NEW SKILLS**

READ MORE BOOKS

**EDUCATION**

small step everyday

*Language School*

learn SOMETHING new EVERYDAY

ONLINE CLASSES

INVEST IN YOURSELF

DON'T COMPARE YOURSELF to OTHERS

# DECIDE
# COMMIT
# FOCUS
# SUCCEED

STAY
STRONG

STUDY NOW
BE PROUD LATER

HAPPY MIND
HAPPY LIFE.

Every
day is a
fresh start

IF YOU CAN
DREAM
IT, YOU
CAN DO IT.

GOOD
VIBES

Dream
big

NO Pain
NO GAIN

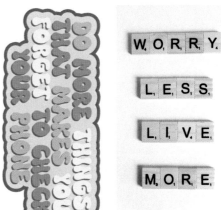

W.O.R.R.Y.

L.E.S.S.

L.I.V.E.

M.O.R.E.

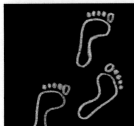
Big journeys
begin with
small steps

BE THE BEST
VERSION
OF YOU !

# ENJOY THE
# LITTLE
# THINGS

Let's PARTY ALL Night

REDUCE REUSE RECYCLE

You Are What You EAT
Vegan

VOLUNTEER

SAVE THE OCEAN

SAY NO to PLASTIC

CHANGE OUR WORLD

DONATION

Make A Difference

DONATE BLOOD

We ♥ our Volunteers

WORK TOGETHER!

ADOPT ME

HELP the HOMELESS

| Career | Love | Marriage |
| Health | Dream Home | Friendship |
| Education | Relax | Volunteering |
| Fitness | Mindfulness | Family |
| Weight Loss | Money | Travel |
| Self-Care | Goals | Hobbies |
| Pet Love | Spiritual | Creativity |
| Happiness | Creativity | Success |
| Abundance | Empowerment | Style |
| Gratitude | Adventure | Learning |
| Dreams | Faith | Marriage |
| Friends | Balance | Growth |
| Independence | Freedom | Sport |

Made in United States
Orlando, FL
30 December 2024

56702771R00029